The Life of
Ben Franklin/

La vida de
Ben Franklin

By Maria Nelson   Traducción al español: Eduardo Alamán

Gareth Stevens
Publishing

Please visit our website, www.garethstevens.com. For a free color catalog of all our high-quality books, call toll free 1-800-542-2595 or fax 1-877-542-2596.

Library of Congress Cataloging-in-Publication Data

Nelson, Maria.
[Life of Ben Franklin. Spanish & English]
The life of Ben Franklin = La vida de Ben Franklin / Maria Nelson.
    p. cm. — (Famous lives = Vidas extraordinarias)
Includes index.
ISBN 978-1-4339-6653-8 (library binding)
1. Franklin, Benjamin, 1706-1790—Juvenile literature. 2. Statesmen—United States—Biography—Juvenile literature. 3. Inventors—United States—Biography—Juvenile literature. 4. Scientists—United States—Biography—Juvenile literature. 5. Printers—United States—Biography—Juvenile literature. I. Title. II. Title: Vida de Ben Franklin.
E302.6.F8N4517 2012
973.3092—dc23
[B]
                                    2011039197

First Edition

Published in 2012 by
Gareth Stevens Publishing
111 East 14th Street, Suite 349
New York, NY 10003

Designer: Daniel Hosek
Editor: Kristen Rajczak
Spanish translation: Eduardo Alamán

Photo credits: Cover, pp. 1, 5, 17, 21 Stock Montage/Getty Images; pp. 7, 9, 11 Kean Collection/ Getty Images; p. 13 Hulton Archive/Getty Images; p. 15 Time Life Pictures/Getty Images; p. 19 Roger Viollet Collection/Getty Images.

Printed in the United States of America

CPSIA compliance information: Batch #CW12GS: For further information contact Gareth Stevens, New York, New York at 1-800-542-2595.

Contents

Contenido

Boldface words appear in the glossary/
Las palabras en **negrita** aparecen en el glosario

Founding Father

Ben Franklin was one of our nation's Founding Fathers. He helped the United States become the country it is today. Ben was a writer, a **diplomat**, and an inventor.

- -

Fundador de la nación

Ben Franklin fue uno de los fundadores de nuestro país. Franklin ayudó a que los Estados Unidos se convirtieran en el país que conocemos hoy. Franklin fue escritor, **diplomático** e inventor.

5

Young Life

Ben was born January 17, 1706. He was one of 17 children! The family lived in Boston, Massachusetts. Ben didn't go to school for very long. He read a lot and taught himself to write well.

Primeros años

Ben nació el 17 de enero de 1706. ¡Ben fue uno de 17 hijos! La familia vivía en Boston, Massachusetts. Ben no fue a la escuela por mucho tiempo. Pero Ben leía mucho y aprendió a escribir muy bien.

When Ben was 12 years old, he worked for his brother James. James was a printer who started a newspaper. Ben wrote **essays** for it. No one knew he wrote them!

A los 12 años, Ben trabajaba con su hermano James. James era impresor y tenía un periódico. Ben escribía **ensayos** para su hermano. ¡Nadie sabía que Ben escribía los ensayos!

9

Ben moved to Philadelphia, Pennsylvania, when he was 17. He worked as a printer. Then, Ben went to London, England. He returned to Philadelphia in 1726. In 1730, he married Deborah Read Rogers.

Ben se mudó a Filadelfia, en Pensilvania, cuando cumplio 17 años. Ahí, trabajó en una imprenta. Luego fue a Londres, Inglaterra. En 1726 regresó a Filadelfia. En 1730 se casó con Deborah Read Rogers.

11

Electricity!

Ben had many interests. He opened the first library in Philadelphia and started a police force. Ben also studied electricity. He discovered many new things about it. His very unsafe **experiment** with a kite is famous.

- -

¡Electricidad!

A Ben le interesaban muchas cosas. Ben abrió la primera biblioteca en Filadelfia y comenzó el departamento de policía. Además, Ben estudió la electricidad. Ben descubrió muchas cosas sobre este tema. Su **experimento** con una cometa, aunque peligroso, es muy famoso.

13

Public Life

Ben respected the British government. He ran for public office during the 1740s and 1750s. However, by the 1760s, many **colonists** were angry with British laws. Ben wrote essays about the colonists' problems.

- -

Vida pública

Ben respetaba al gobierno británico. Durante las décadas de 1740 y 1750, Ben compitió por trabajar en el gobierno. Sin embargo, para los años 1760, los **colonos** estaban molestos con las leyes británicas. Ben escribió ensayos sobre los problemas de los colonos.

15

In 1776, Ben helped write the **Declaration of Independence**. He was then sent to France. Ben was very popular there. He asked the French to help the colonists fight British rule.

- -

En 1776, Ben ayudó a escribir la **Declaración de Independencia**. Ben fue enviado a Francia, donde fue muy popular. Ben le pidió a los franceses que pelearan contra el control de los británicos.

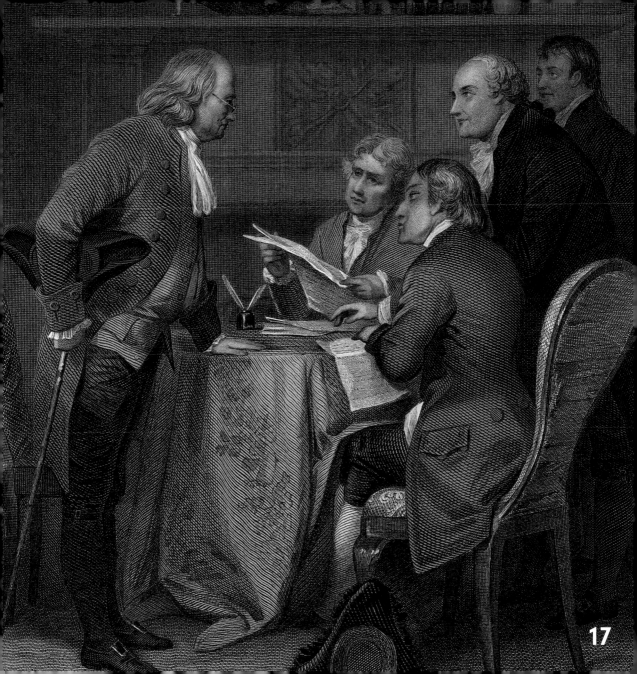

A New Country

In 1783, the United States won its independence!
Ben helped work out a peace agreement with
England. Then, he helped write the **US Constitution**
in 1787. It stated the new country's laws.

Una nueva nación

¡En 1783, los Estados Unidos ganaron su
independencia! Ben ayudó a escribir un acuerdo
de paz con Inglaterra. Luego, ayudó a escribir la
Constitución de los Estados Unidos en 1787. La
constitución estableció las leyes de la nueva nación.

19

Inventor

Ben died in 1790. However, his inventions live on. Ben invented many things, including a special kind of glasses and a stove. Today, he is remembered for these and for helping shape the United States.

Inventor

Ben murió en 1790. Sin embargo, sus inventos siguen vivos. Ben inventó muchas cosas, incluidos unos lentes especiales y una estufa. Hoy es recordado por sus inventos y por ayudar en la formación de los Estados Unidos.

Timeline/Cronologiá

1706 — Ben Franklin is born on January 17./Ben Franklin nace el 17 de enero.

1730 — Ben marries Deborah Read Rogers./Ben se casa con Deborah Read Rogers.

1776 — Ben helps write the Declaration of Independence./Ben ayuda a escribir la Declaración de Independencia.

1787 — Ben helps write the US Constitution./Ben ayuda a escribir la Constitución de EE.UU.

1790 — Ben dies./Ben muere.

Glossary/Glosario

colonist: someone who lives in a colony, or a piece of land under the control of another country

Declaration of Independence: the piece of writing that stated the colonies' wish to form their own government without British control

diplomat: a person who is skilled at talks between nations

essay: a piece of writing

experiment: a test that tries out a new idea

US Constitution: the piece of writing stating the laws of the United States

- -

colono: persona que vive en una colonia, o territorio controlado por otro país.

Constitución de los Estados Unidos (la): el documento que establece las leyes de este país.

Declaración de Independencia (la): el documento que decía que las colonias querían formar un gobierno sin el control de los británicos.

diplomático, a (el/la): persona que representa a una nación.

ensayo (el): una forma de escritura.

experimento (el): algo que prueba una nueva idea.

For More Information/Más información

Books/Libros

Barretta, Gene. *Now & Ben: The Modern Inventions of Benjamin Franklin.* New York, NY: Henry Holt and Co., 2009.

Schroeder, Alan. *Ben Franklin: His Wit and Wisdom from A to Z.* New York, NY: Holiday House, 2011.

Web Sites/Páginas en Internet

Benjamin Franklin

bensguide.gpo.gov/benfranklin/

Read more about Ben Franklin's inventions and his work for the United States.

Name That Founding Father

www.history.org/kids/games/foundingFather.cfm

Play a game to learn more about the Founding Fathers.

Index/Índice